Dickens: The Later Novels

by BARBARA HARDY

Published for the British Council
and the National Book League
by Longmans, Green & Co

Distributed by
The British Book Centre
Elmsford   New York

In recent years there has been a revaluation of Dickens's fiction and most critics now consider his late novels to be his greatest achievements. In this essay, Barbara Hardy considers the last seven novels from *Bleak House* (1857) to his final, unfinished novel, *Edwin Drood*.

All the later novels, with the exception of *A Tale of Two Cities*, present a criticism of the institutions of Victorian England. Against a background of riots and mounting fear of revolution, Dickens's attack on capitalist society becomes more urgent and passionate, and this urgency creates novels of greater compactness and concentration. As Dickens 'explores more bleakly a bleaker world' there are fewer jokes and the comedy becomes harsher. In these novels of the sociological imagination there is also a developing sense of character, an interest in the inner life of such characters as Louisa in *Hard Times*, Clennam in *Little Dorrit* and Pip in *Great Expectations*.

'The central and continuing interest revealed by all his novels,' writes Barbara Hardy, 'is his divided concern with individual love and moral success, on the other hand, and social heartlessness and breakdown on the other', a duality which becomes more pronounced in the later novels.

Barbara Hardy is Professor of English Language and Literature at Royal Holloway College, University of London. She is the author of *The Novels of George Eliot* and *The Appropriate Form* and has edited *Middlemarch: Critical Approaches to the Novel* and *Daniel Deronda*.

The bibliography in this essay as in *Dickens: The Early Novels* (No 204) is reprinted, with minor additions, from Professor Fielding's *Dickens* (No 37 in the series).

Bibliographical Series
of Supplements to 'British Book News'
on Writers and Their Work

★

GENERAL EDITOR
Geoffrey Bullough

CHARLES DICKENS

THE LATER NOVELS

Bleak House . Hard Times . Little Dorrit
A Tale of Two Cities . Great Expectations
Our Mutual Friend . Edwin Drood

by

BARBARA HARDY

PUBLISHED FOR
THE BRITISH COUNCIL
AND THE NATIONAL BOOK LEAGUE
BY LONGMANS, GREEN & CO

99393

LONGMANS, GREEN & CO. LTD.
48 Grosvenor Street, London, W1

*Associated companies, branches and
representatives throughout the world*

First published 1968
© Barbara Hardy 1968

Printed in Great Britain by
F. Mildner & Sons, London, EC1

CONTENTS

Charles Dickens was born on 7 February 1812 at Portsmouth. He died on 9 June 1870 at Gad's Hill, Kent, and was buried in Westminster Abbey.

CHARLES DICKENS:
THE LATER NOVELS

I. THE CONTINUITY OF DICKENS

THIS essay will be devoted to the seven novels which form the last half of Dickens's work, but I wish to begin by saying something about those aspects of his mind and art which are not confined to any one period. First, there is his comedy. This is an important aspect of his uniqueness, more often praised than dwelt on. Dickens's power as a comic writer changes, both in its nature and its relation to his compassion, his social criticism and his actions, but it never dies. In his very last completed novel, *Our Mutual Friend,* we find Mrs Wilfer, a ludicrously funny character, closely related to the moral analysis of marriage and money but rousing laughter by a gloriously unaware self-display which takes us right back to Mrs Nickleby. Mrs Nickleby is a freer comic character, not so involved in a moral criticism, but cast in a very similar mould. If we see the continuity of Dickens's comic characters we are forced also to recognize his creation of individuality: stock they may be, both outside Dickens and within, but his great talent as a creator of comic character seems to lie in the rare fusion of caricature, which is simple, diagrammatic, exaggerated, with personality, which is mobile, animated and particular. Only in *Pickwick Papers* did he create static caricature, and even there we can find him learning the nature of comedy as the novel progresses, as he leaves empty farce and flat humours for the particularity and *verve* of Sam Weller, who scatters his spirit all round.

One chief source of his comic animation is the ventriloquial use of language, learnt from the eighteenth-century novelists, especially Smollett, and from contemporary music-hall, but used in the proliferation of styles that are

expressive and wild, imitative and fantastic. Comedy becomes more and more sober in late Dickens, more and more
directed towards satire, but even in the early novels we find
the special Dickensian blending and matching of comic
characters and language with the characters and language
of a serious and even pathetic style. From *Oliver Twist*
onward, there are cunning and heart-catching modulations
from comedy to pathos, from gleeful delight in farce or
ridicule to sober reflection. I say 'cunning and heart-
catching' because another strange and unchanging quality
in Dickens is his ability to manipulate our sympathies, and
very frankly and openly, without losing them. It is often
said that, if we see the mechanism, the spell ceases to work.
It is very hard to apply *this* principle of perception to
Dickens. In the first chapter of *Oliver Twist* we are shifted
with uncomfortable rapidity from the humours of the
drunken old woman, to the pathos of the young dying
mother, to the satire of officialdom. In a famous episode
from *Dombey and Son* we turn our head, sentence by
sentence, from Paul's strange intense description of those
visionary waves to the bewildered literal questioning of
Toots. Even when we see what Dickens is doing, it is very
difficult to resist the sway of such rapid motion and modu-
lation. It is difficult to stay unsympathetic to intensity, or
too closely identified with it, and such rapid switches help
in all the novels to hold together a dense and various
emotional action, to provide the relief of variety and
continuity of attention, and to give Dickens's talent the
double opportunity for comedy and pathos, combining
with each other and controlling each other. Such juxtapositions are less startling in the later novels, where the
comedy tends to grow more satirical, more tightly related
to the central ideas, but they are still present. There is the
horrifying juxtaposition of Chadband's gross appetite and
gross language with the frailty of Jo, his text and object.
There is the tense farce of Mrs Sparsit's tracking-down of
Louisa Bounderby in the storm. There is Sloppy's dismal

howl of gratitude for Mrs Boffin's kindness, immediately drowned in the comic enquiry of the footman who looks in because he 'thought it was Cats'. And there are even more closely woven fabrics made up of threads of the grim and the comic, as in the episode of Mr Merdle's suicide. Sometimes the juxtapositions and mixtures are determinedly critical: the pity we feel for Jo is created out of the contemptuous laughter roused by Chadband, and Mrs Sparsit's delight in Louisa's desperate misery is comically punished as her bonnet is reduced to 'an overripe fig' and she is covered by 'stagnant verdure'. The juxtapositions are usually exercising control: where comedy and pathos, or comedy and grim melodrama, go hand-in-hand, there is little danger of Dickens falling into the lengthy lachrymose vein of some of the worst flights in *Oliver Twist* and *The Old Curiosity Shop*, and I think it fair to say that the control increases as his art matures. But it is also true, as I see it, that Dickens grows cleverer in his rendering of emotion rather than more sensitive in the actual emotion. He rushes us away from Sloppy's undying gratitude in a diplomatic and rather mechanical fashion. His presentation of gratitude, love, pity, constancy and so on is often crude, thin and stereotyped, and the presence of comedy cleverly disguises such crudity and thinness, suggests a built-in criticism and relief, divides up the intensities so that we are not allowed to stay with them long enough to be disgusted, suspicious and alienated. What Dickens lacks in sensitivity and subtlety of feeling is *almost* made up by his craft and cunning.

Dickens's weakness in imagination, from the beginning to the end of his writing, lies in the area of the emotions, and especially the tender emotions. Since his rhetoric is very immediately persuasive and appealing, and since his art is a highly moral art that depends on the creation of ideals of virtue, this banality of feeling remains a serious disadvantage. He can be crudely highflown, over-solemn and cosily complacent. I can see no very important distinction between the emotions he canvasses on behalf of his early heroines and his late. Rose Maylie, Nell, Florence Dombey, Agnes, Esther Summerson and—with much greater success —even Little Dorrit are presented in order to move us by compassion and admiration. All are ideals of domestic proficiency and concentrated virtue that have happily dated. They are still sometimes defended on the grounds that their identity is symbolic rather than realistic and related to fairy-tale or myth rather than to the imitation of life. It is obviously—very obviously—true that they are presented in fairy-tale and fabulous terms, but this only serves to draw attention to their sentimentality. Genuinely resonant myth-ological characters, such as Cinderella, Kafka's 'K' or Beckett's tramps, make their appeal by tapping our collec-tive awareness, and do not need to be fussed over and advertised. Dickens's heroines are propped up by fairy-tale references (as real fairy-tale characters never are) and are also surrounded by emotional demands: they are too much admired, too much loved, too much pitied, too much held up as emotional stimuli. A symbolic character like Cinderella makes her point by the simplicity and singularity of the situation: if we try to imagine the teller of her tale asking for pity and admiration the difference between fairy-tale symbolism, and Dickens's sentimental idealization, should be plain.

This is not to say that Dickens could not particularize character. His characters do tend to succeed, however, in direct proportion to their grotesqueness, though there are the two exceptions of the young David and Pip. Dickens's ability to throw himself with an actor's energy into fan-tasies, on the stage, in life and in writing, shows itself at its best in bizarre creation, though it is also his need of fantasy's healing-power that may have made him particularly vulnerable to the artistic temptation to create in order to solve and gratify. His model heroines are probably indulgent creations of this order, though it is worth noticing that they do not utterly disappear after he met Ellen Ternan, in 1857: Lucie Manette, Biddy, Bella and Lizzie, and Rosa Bud

celebrate different aspects of his feminine model, and only
Biddy and perhaps Lizzie are really defensible creations. His
later heroines of more originality and spirit, like Estella and
Helena Landless, are sometimes seen as images of Ellen
Ternan, but he had in fact created similar women characters
earlier, in *Dombey and Son* and *Hard Times*, where Edith and
Louisa show Dickens's possession and expression of some
subtle insights into female sexuality, pride and aggressive-
ness, before meeting Ellen Ternan. As Professor Fielding
pointed out in his pamphlet on Dickens (*Writers and Their
Work*, No 37), no one has really used recent biographical
revelations in the criticism of the novels in a way which is
precise and definite. A correlation best not attempted in the
chronology of his novels is the simple and dubious correlation between the life he was leading and the books he
was writing. Even the domestic ideal that we can rather
easily see as a compensating fantasy for discontent was after
all part of his environment and, as in his other apparently
indulgent fantasies drawn from religion and a Romantic
view of nature, it is by no means easy to see what has
personal roots and what is literary imitation—and what is
both.

To my mind, the central and continuing interest revealed
by all his novels is his divided concern with individual love
and moral success, on the one hand, and social heartlessness
and breakdown on the other. We find this duality very
tensely giving shape to the last novels, but it is also present
much earlier. He saw both Oliver and Nell, for instance, as
representing virtue and innocence in a grotesquely malevo-
lent world. They are victims, exposed to much and
threatened by more, and we tread their tightrope of danger.
They are triumphant hero and heroine, and we celebrate
the powers of love in a world governed by the unloving.
The optimism that creates Oliver and Nell and their happy
triumphs (Nell's death in no way removes the triumph, but
gives her a kind of sham apotheosis) is linked with a world
which is more easily defeated than it is in the later novels,

where the images of optimism cohabit with a much darker social imagery. Moreover, Dickens becomes more detailed and documentary in his portraits of society. It is true that the underworld of *Oliver Twist* is nasty, violent and dirty, and that the wanderings of Nell and her grandfather take them through dark ways in rough company. But in spite of the topicality of the criticism of the New Poor Law in *Oliver Twist*, and the topicality of the threatening industrial hells in *The Old Curiosity Shop*, neither novel makes a large-scale and detailed attack on the country, the system, the establishment and their values as the later novels so insistently, variously, and lucidly do. The sociological imagination of Dickens comes fully to life in his later novels. We cannot there feel that the workhouse and the slum provide an appropriate environment for the fable of evil struggling to destroy goodness: we have to feel that workhouses, slums, filthy graveyards, poverty and servitude are all related to each other, and are permitted and created by stately homes, comfortable living, ceremony, wealth and privilege, which are also all related to each other. The social analysis is on a large scale, and this means that it *is* an analysis. No doubt Dickens was moved to criticise the workhouse and the baby-farm in *Oliver Twist*, but in the novels from *Bleak House* onwards (and one should indeed look back and include *Dombey and Son*) Dickens may choose to centre attention on a special institution, but always insistently places it in relation to other institutions. Because of this totality of analysis the later Dickens arrives at a rather different relation between his individual principle of love and his picture of loveless society. It was easier to argue (explicitly, but chiefly by the powerful implicit persuasive showing of art) that what the workhouses and baby-farms lacked was love, love like the love of Oliver or Brownlow, and to suggest remedy at the same time as diagnosis, than it was to argue that what England in the 'fifties needed was more loving people. This is of course putting the relationship between the picture of society and the picture of the loving individual with deliberate crudeness, but when we turn to the actual novels it is necessary to be more detailed and less crude. In this introductory section I want merely to suggest, that the combination of optimism about people and realism about societies is present from the beginning but not fully revealed and exposed until *Bleak House* and its successors.

II.   CHARACTERISTICS OF LATE DICKENS

As the craft matures, there are technical developments which show themselves in a greater power of control, a tighter handling of narrative form and a proliferation of experiment. It is much easier to see the maturing of a craft than the maturing of a man, and I would not myself argue that Dickens's insights into the human heart and the workings of human institutions became more profound and certain. He remains an optimist, at least in his art, though the optimism of his conclusions and implications becomes in certain ways darkened and muted. If everything we can say about the development of his art might be said also of the later writing of a good many novelists, so we can also say that Dickens is scarcely singular in a certain loss of cheerfulness and exhilaration.

What differences are there between the first and the second half of his work? Putting it in terms of two halves is of course arbitrary, and we might choose to divide his career into an apprenticeship lasting until, say, the completion of *Martin Chuzzlewit* in 1844 and a later period of maturity. Some people would prefer to take the apprenticeship up to the completion of *David Copperfield* in 1850. I do not think that the concept of apprenticeship and mastery is a very useful or appropriate one to use when writing about Dickens: a very early novel, *Oliver Twist*, seems to me as controlled and proficient as *Bleak House*, and while we should all agree that there are flaws of feeling in *The Old*

Curiosity Shop, we should be hard put to deny the existence of very similar flaws in *Hard Times* and *A Tale of Two Cities*. We might make the division rather differently, without thinking in terms of immaturity and maturity, uncertainty and certainty, but of a clarity and ordering of ideas, and then we might well see early Dickens ending with *Martin Chuzzlewit* in 1844, taking the cue from Dickens himself when he saw it as the analysis of selfishness and said he intended to attempt such a unity of moral design and idea in all his future novels.

The advantage of beginning the later period with *Bleak House*, for all its admitted arbitrariness, is that it does group together a *fairly* homogeneous collection of novels. They are all novels of the sociological imagination: while no one would deny the social concern and analysis of the earlier novels, there are some, like *Martin Chuzzlewit* and *David Copperfield*, which deal only loosely or obliquely with contemporary England, but all the novels I am calling 'late', with the exception of *A Tale of Two Cities*, set out a full map and a large-scale criticism, in the expressive form of art, of Dickens's England. We could be more precise than this: each of the late novels creates a form which animates social analysis, while at the same time representing the power and fragile strength of the individual human heart, to which Dickens, like George Eliot or D. H. Lawrence, pinned his hopes. We could say that Dickens is imitating the action of institutions: in *Bleak House* it is the institution of the Law, in *Little Dorrit* of the Prison, in *Great Expectations* and *Our Mutual Friend* it is Class; in *Hard Times* it is Education, and even in the more obliquely critical *A Tale of Two Cities* it is Revolution. This is a crude diagram which should make all Dickens readers demur: of course the institutions I have capitalized so dramatically are merely the special cases brought to the fore in each novel. Dickens may not have been as sophisticated a political thinker as some Marxists have made out, but he was sophisticated enough to see all these institutions as characteristic of capitalist society.

And all his novels in this period are concerned with the confrontation of the rich and the poor, the privileged and the unprivileged, the gentle and the rough, capital and labour. Remembering that from the mid-'sixties onwards, there was depression, riot, and the genuine fear of revolution in England, it is perhaps not surprising that Dickens's concern with social criticism becomes more passionate, more urgent, more sharply and wholly the shaping force in the novels.

I want to stress the words 'shaping force'. I am here concerned with the form as well as the subject of his later novels, believing that the two are inseparable, though the terms in which I have just been describing the art may sound more appropriate to social criticism not cast in the form of fiction. I think it is this urgent feeling about the condition of England which conditions the tighter and tauter forms of these novels. From the point of view of an elegant formalist like Henry James, who disliked multiple plots and a mass of particulars, these novels are very far from being tight and taut, are indeed instances of what James called 'large loose baggy monsters'. But if we compare them with the rambling form of *Pickwick Papers*, *Nicholas Nickleby*, *The Old Curiosity Shop*, and even *David Copperfield*—all novels which reveal the strong influence of Dickens's beloved Smollett and Fielding—the concentration becomes very plain. This is not to say that they are necessarily better novels, by the way, nor that the early novels I mention are too loose or too episodic: most of them achieve sufficient unity in spite of the looseness and all of them achieve individual effects through the very existence of such looseness. But the late novels are not loose, and what gives them their binding concentration, I suggest, is the insistent analysis of society.

Like all novels, they are about people. Like most novels, they create characters. Like many novels, they seem to need one character on whom interest and feeling is focussed. And we could say that these novels are linked not only by their concentrated social criticism, but that they achieve a greater intensity of psychological interest too, that their heroes and heroines are more wholly and strongly in the centre. This is not quite true of *Hard Times* or *A Tale of Two Cities* (novels published in weekly instalments) but it is true of all the others. In *Bleak House* there is Esther Summerson; in *Little Dorrit* there is Dorrit; in *Great Expectations* there is Pip. It may very well be objected that some of these characters share the interest and intensity of the novel with other developed characters, and this is true. When I speak of the heroes and heroines being more wholly and strongly in the centre, I am thinking of their peculiar relation to the social landscape of the novel: each of these characters is related to the world of their novel, a world which bears an imaginative resemblance to Dickens's own society, as a symbol and instance of special humane faith: they are at once victims and resilient heroes. Once more, I must blur the lines of my own distinctions: we might say the same of Oliver and Little Nell and Barnaby, though not, I think, of the heroes and heroines of any of the other early novels. Each of the qualities I am picking out as character-istic of the late novels may be found here and there in the early period: what I am pointing to is not the emergence of any single new quality but a greater degree of homogeneity amongst the novels themselves.

They explore more bleakly a bleaker world. It is neces-sary, I think, to put the bleakness in adverbial and adjectival form. Dickens had a surprising capacity to transform dark-ness by setting off comic fireworks in his early novels. Many of the energetic jokes that spray *Pickwick Papers* with vitality and humour are sick jokes, turning poverty, disease, servitude and death into the comic anecdote and the comic scene. Take, for instance, Sam Weller's jokes about the servant-girl taking laudanum, Jingle's joke about drains, the comic action of the medical students eating voraciously and discussing the dissection of a child. Dickens ceases to make this kind of joke. I am most certainly not arguing that he improved therefore in taste, or sensibility, or tact, but merely observing that his comic range grew more limited, and that this narrowing-down of range makes the later novels bleaker and darker. You cannot imagine a joke about sanitation in *Bleak House*, where it is a social problem, treated imaginatively and sensuously, moving us through pity and disgust and creating an effective symbol out of an actual social illustration, physically realized. You cannot imagine a joke about disease in *Bleak House*, or about a servant-girl, or a child's death.

But not merely is the range narrower, so that Dickens treats the subjects that once he had been able to treat comically in a harsh satire or intense compassion. So also is the amount of comedy smaller: there are very few jokes, there are relatively few comic scenes, there are comic characters, but they often turn out to have a serious intent. And the comedy is less free: there are practically no zany episodes like Mr Pecksniff's inebriation, or wild speeches, like Mrs Gamp's recollections of her departed husband. Pecksniff and Mrs Gamp were involved in the analysis of selfishness in *Martin Chuzzlewit*, but they were also centres of comic release, where Dickens could take off into a fantasy-world of bizarre acts and bizarre languages. Such centres are absent in the late novels. The comedy is very largely satiric, harsh and seldom merry. It is sometimes— but very rarely—gentle, as in the creation of Flora Finching in *Little Dorrit*, which reminds us of the generous charm of the Micawbers. Dickens's laughter ceases to be free: it becomes constantly inhibited by the consciousness of the unfunny side of life. In *Oliver Twist* he spoke, in a shrewd and vivid passage, of the likeness his novels bore to the structure of melodrama, where the comic and the serious alternated like the strips of fat and lean in 'streaky bacon'. We can still find the alternation of the comic and the serious in these novels of the 'fifties and 'sixties, but it is more like the kind of streaky bacon where the fat is pink and the lean pale: the comic and the serious blend into each, make for a closer unity of the separate parts and effects of the novel. The impurity of the comedy, its inhibited and harsh nature, is another source of that sense of greater concentration which we find in this period.

III.   THE LATE NOVELS

Bleak House was published in monthly parts, beginning in March 1852. It is one of the most thoroughly researched of Dickens's novels, and scholars have collated the fiction with the facts of history, and concluded that this is a highly topical novel, in its Carlylean symbolism of fire and fog, and its documentary materials. 'Documentary' is a misleading word: Dickens was a novelist, not only a reporter, and he took such contemporary events and problems as the Manning case, a *cause célèbre* which was the source for the murder-story, the charitable efforts of Mrs Chisholm's Family Colonisation Society, the Oxford Movement, violently and irreverently parodied in Mrs Pardiggle and her unfortunate sons, scandals about sanitation and cholera, and the criticism and all-too-slow reform of Chancery, and joined them together in invention and connection. The invention allowed him to fit his historical materials together, but the combination also comes out of a sense of the need to connect apparently discrete events and institutions in society. Chancery and a great house and the brickmakers and the frightful slums of Tom All Alone's are closely connected: rank and wealth and ease is responsible for ignorance and poverty and pain. And if the reason will not see and accept such connections, the body will be forced to—the disease which does not know its place will act as a violent physiological metaphor for the oneness of the body politic. The fog is of course commonly celebrated as the controlling image of the novel, but it is really only one instance and aspect of that bleakness announced in the title, a bleakness which is cold, wet, filthy. The house of England exposes its citizens to cruel weathers. Cold, wet, fog and dirt are sensuously explored throughout a novel which not only makes us laugh, cry and wait, in the manner of the advice Dickens gave to Wilkie Collins, but also makes us feel and smell. From the very beginning of the novel, with the present tense of a verbless bird's-eye view of the Thames and London, we move through strongly sensuous experiences. The fog's chill and blur are felt and seen—and, indeed, the beginning of the novel would be very thinly and obviously allegorical if this were not so, for most of the equations and interpretations drawn by the critics are also drawn most explicitly by Dickens himself. Some readers have understandably felt Dickens's loud explicitness to be an irritant: he leaves little to be subtly inferred but states and restates, puts the case at the top of his voice, repeats it in capital letters, and then adds an extra gloss in a footnote. Dickens's novels were listened to by groups of illiterates as Thackeray's and George Eliot's never were, and their popularity and accessibility is sometimes lost sight of today, when their lengthiness, weight of description and sheer Victorian ponderousness of style may make them seem difficult to inexperienced readers. Although his symbolism may strike the experienced reader as too explicit, we still participate actively through the sensuous dimension. We move through the novel feeling fog, damp, filth and slime, and when the sensations of revulsion are held up by Esther's orderly housekeeping or Chadband's *gourmet* delights, the interruptions are pointed. Dickens animates his schematic symbol, and involves us in a close and concrete relation with places, events and characters. Like his Fat Boy in *Pickwick*, he wants to make our flesh creep by the contaminating exposures of *Bleak House*.

He moves us through disgust and pity, but also through comedy. Most of it is satirically articulate. Mrs Jellyby, Mr Turveydrop, the Pardiggles, Chadband, and Harold Skimpole are contemptuously ridiculed instances of heartless and happy survivals amongst so many victims. The character of Mrs Bayham Badger, whose distinguished ex-husbands are proudly paraded by her present spouse, is the nearest we get to a flight of pure comedy:

'Mrs Badger has been married to three husbands—two of them highly distinguished men,' said Mr Badger, summing up the facts; 'and, each time, upon the twenty-first of March at eleven in the forenoon!'

This has the old wild touch of superfluous detail, and though Mrs Badger is another type of solipsist seclusion and survival, and her best scene carefully placed before the passage revealing the love of Ada and Richard, it has a gaiety which is rare in this dark novel. The grimness of satire is sustained in the rhetoric and language of the omniscient narrator who shares the story-telling with Esther. The language used is often hortatory, even forensic. The reader is addressed and pressed, often in the manner of a prosecuting counsel, judge, or interrogator persuading, accusing, questioning, informing, summing up. The range of tone and feeling in this cross-examination is considerable. There is dry irony: 'Mr Vholes is a very respectable man. He has not a large business, but he is a very respectable man. He is allowed by the greater attorneys who have made good fortunes, or are making them, to be a most respectable man'; and acid astringency: 'The one great principle of the English law is, to make business for itself'. The voice can lose both dryness and irony in passionate vituperation, as when the present tense loses finite verbs as on the occasion of Jo's death:

Dead, your Majesty. Dead, my lords and gentlemen. Dead, Right Reverends and Wrong Reverends of every order. Dead, men and women, born with Heavenly compassion in your hearts. And dying thus around us every day.

The stark descriptions and direct address of this narration in the present is of course contrasted with the placid tones of Esther's narrative. One of her many disadvantages as narrator/heroine is her total lack of edge, irony, or humour, a disadvantage she shares with other virtuous models in Dickens and George Eliot, but which is peculiarly marked and limiting because she is a storyteller contrasted with the flexibility and force of another storyteller. Dickens is of course making an enterprising experiment in narrative structure, and the best account of this can be found in W. J. Harvey's essay in *Dickens and the Twentieth Century*. We move significantly from the limited vision and feeling of Esther to the larger darker vision unattached to 'I', whose detachment is underlined by the present tense which bleakly records the way things are. The detachment has both passion and judgment, and is rather like the detachment one would expect of a recording angel. But the division between the two narratives makes particularly plain that awkward duality of vision between the optimistic record of the individual heart and the black record of society.

Esther's story shows the energy of virtue and its final happy success; the social record shows the energy of destructive injustice. We are left with the constructiveness of the good housekeeper and the good doctor, rewarded with each other, cosily settled in their rustic version of 'Bleak House', whose 'doll's rooms' strike some readers as an impropriety after Tom All Alone's. True, Dickens disturbs the final harmony with the discords of Caddy's deaf-and-dumb child and Ada's mourning, but the strongest chords are those expressing peace, beauty restored, pain soothed, virtue recognized, energy activated, the wind never in the east. Dickens does not seem to be making his final passages ironical, and we are asked to move from the powerful indictment to this weak doll's-house conclusion. It is not just that Dickens tends to use the conventional happy ending, but—I suggest—that such an ending reveals his own divided mind. He found it possible to feel boundless hope in the human heart, none in societies and institutions. As soon as loving impulse becomes institutionalized into charity, at least in this novel (certainly not in *A Christmas Carol*) it kills the love of individuals by individuals. And it is understandable if depressing to find that the conclusion to the novel seems to expect so much congratulation. The reconciliation is too tiny, too unrepresentative, to act as an exit from our total experience of this novel. The sense of narrowing is increased by Esther's unreality: if there is indeed hope to be found in human hearts, let them be more complex and more eroded by experience than Miss Summerson's. Her symbolic name and fairy-tale associations with Dame Durden and the rest do not make her a character with genuine mythological weight, but reveal their inadequacy in a context of solicitation, indulgence, admiration, modest under-statement and complacency. Some of these feelings which the author demands for the heroine are made especially unavailable because of her role as narrator. We can only be glad that it was David and not Agnes who told the story of *David Copperfield*.

In the next few novels Dickens seems to take pains to avoid this kind of duality and partial reconciliation. *Hard Times*, *Little Dorrit*, *A Tale of Two Cities* and *Great Expectations* make concluding demands on the reader which are appropriately limited and have no suggestion of expecting us to settle down and see everything and everyone as now likely to do nicely after all that pain. The sense of reality is something that starts at the beginnings of *Hard Times* (1854) with a certain toughening of the moral humours in the two chief women characters. Sissy Jupes is a more subdued type of the female heart than Esther, and we are moreover asked to concentrate not on Sissy but on Louisa, a very interesting study in moral psychology who also makes limited demands on our credulity and our faith. Like Edith Dombey, to whom she is obviously related, Louisa is a case of repressed passion and vision. She sees the highest but pride and self-contempt drive her into following the lowest. Out of an interesting mixture of shame and doubt she perversely represses her capacity for virtue and tries to act out the utilitarian disregard for feeling which her education has held up as a model. She does not follow Edith's earlier course of self-punishing and male-punishing action, and is indeed actually moved by Harthouse (and he by her, and by Sissy) as Edith never is by Carker. Harthouse is indeed a less stagey and very compressed new version of Carker, a study in perverted *ennui* who is a sketch for Eugene Wrayburn. Louisa is also exposed to experience not simply as a victim, like Esther Summerson, but as a susceptible and malleable human being who has a capacity for damnation. Though the treatment of the working-class characters and industrial problems is sentimental, thin, and crass, the virtue of *Hard Times* lies in a new kind of truthfulness about social conditioning of character. We do not find the anatomy of destructiveness followed by a small-scale model of construction as in *Bleak House*. The humours of the self-made man *gloriosus*, in Bounderby, and of the convertible Utilitarian, in Gradgrind, are incisive and spirited, very much in the manner of those Jonsonian humours whose very narrowness produces a pressure of vitality. The presentation of the circus with its symbols of pastime, joy and goodhearted sleaziness is effective within the limits of the fable and, in spite of its embarrassing lisping innocence, responds adequately enough to the counter-symbol of the fact-choked and fact-choking schoolroom. The novel certainly lacks a proper adult paradigm for the imaginative and sensual life denied by Gradgrind, but so much of the focus is on the child's education that this almost passes without notice. That it does not pass quite without notice is perhaps a tribute to the delineation of passion, repression and conflict in Louisa. Dickens cannot really be said to explore her inner life, but he manages very skilfully, as he did with Dombey, to imply it.

Louisa does not go right down to the bottom of Mrs Sparsit's imaged moral staircase, but her redemption is treated with some sternness and there is no falsely triumphant climax. The anatomy of a heartless education and a heartless industrialism, linked by the criterion of efficiency, concludes with no more than a sad and sober appraisal:

> Herself again a wife—a mother—lovingly watchful of her children, ever careful that they should have a childhood of the mind no less than a childhood of the body, as knowing it to be even a more beautiful thing, and a possession, any hoarded scrap of which, is a blessing and · happiness to the wisest? Did Louisa see this? Such a thing was never to be.

The last words to the Dear Reader, though discussing the possibility of remedy, is free from optimistic flights: 'It rests with you and me, whether, in our two fields of action, similar things shall be or not'. Dickens looks forward to rebirth—in the lives of children still unborn and in deathbed repentance—but he denies Louisa a brave new life, and the quiet and almost matter-of-fact language makes a true and whole response to the experience of the novel. His capacity for loud cheers and crescendos at the end is subdued, and he suggests that Louisa's future will be undertaken 'as part of no fantastic vow, or bond, or sisterhood . . . but simply as a duty to be done.' It is particularly satisfying that Dickens avoids the pendulum-swing so grossly offensive in *Bleak House,* and does not move into the language and symbolism of strong feeling and vivid fancy in reaction to the world and values of hard fact. He matches heartless rationality with a rational warmth. The very last words of the novel are placed in the context of age and death, which controls the hopefulness: 'We shall sit with lighter bosoms on the hearth, to see the ashes of our fires turn grey and cold.' The image of grey ashes is wholly sensitive to the experience of Coketown, and admits its existence, in contrast to the way that Esther's little Bleak House depended on ignoring the larger bleakness.

Little Dorrit (1857) is a bigger and more complex venture than *Hard Times,* but the new sensibility and toughness remains and grows. Dorrit herself is no complex psychological study, but a very effective character who manages to be both symbolic and sufficiently a creature of time and place. She has a certain grotesqueness—a stuntedness and sexlessness—which helps both to stylize her character as an image of virtue and to make her a more natural prison-child. She is Dickens's most successfully heroic character since Oliver Twist. And she is helped by sharing the interest of the novel with Arthur Clennam, victim of another kind of imprisonment, and a character with more inner life than we have found up to now. He too is responsively and convincingly stunted by environment, and extricates himself slowly and exhaustedly. The virtue and energy Dickens celebrates in this novel is hard-won and battered. Here too the ending is triumphant only in a muted way, and has a rational sobriety and a lack of crescendo. Arthur and Dorrit, like Louisa, move into a 'modest' life. The last sentence of the novel, one of the most sensitive Dickens ever wrote, calls strongly on our sympathies but makes no attempt to wipe out our recollections of all that has happened. It is responsive to the restlessness, dissatisfactions and irresoluteness that have marked so much of the action:

They went quietly down into the roaring streets, inseparable and blessed; and as they passed along in sunshine and shade, the noisy and the eager, and the arrogant and the froward and the vain, fretted and chafed, and made their usual uproar.

The whole novel is not written or imagined with such rational and complex control. There are flights of pity and ecstasy where Dickens is at his worst. When the Dorrit brothers die, for instance, Dickens has some excellent individual touches of act and feeling, in the account of the old man sending off his trinkets and clothing to be pawned, and some striking imagery for death: 'quietly, quietly, the lines of the plan of the great Castle melted'. But he moves off into the banalities of prayer—an act of feeling he simply cannot touch—and into a paradisal imagery which rings loud and hollow: 'The two brothers were before their Father; far beyond the twilight judgments of this world;

high above its mists and obscurities'. Some of the appeals on behalf of Dorrit's frailty and goodness also fall into banality. I emphasize such sentimental patches because I do not want to imply that the late Dickens is entirely in control of himself, his characters and his readers. There is sentimentality, but it is not used to solve problems, reach conclusions and attempt a grandiose finality.

Little Dorrit is like *Bleak House* in its centripetal symbolism. The novelist draws our attention at almost every point to the insistent symbol of imprisonment. When we have mentioned the dark stench of the French prison, with dazzling light outside, and its microcosmic image of class and power; the travellers in quarantine, talking explicitly of prison; the Marshalsea; Dorrit's conceit of the grand European tour which is so like imprisonment; the blatant but striking comparison of the St Bernard hostel to a prison; Mrs Clennam's room and repressive religion, we have made no observations which the novelist does not make repeatedly and clearly for us. The scene has widened: England was like a Bleak House, human life and civilization is like a prison. Perhaps the sensuous life of the symbolism in *Bleak House* is missing here. The prison symbolism is more thinly intellectual, more obviously worked-out in simple equations, though it has a dimension of feeling, perhaps shown most vividly in the depression and restricted energies of Clennam, a prisoner almost incapable of stretching and moving into life. There is the disadvantage that Dickens, like Henry James, makes the characters themselves do so much of the symbol-making, and this is not only an increase in tiring explicitness but at times less than plausible.

The most successful piece of institutional animation has nothing to do with the prison, but presents the Civil Service, then the citadel of ease and privilege, unassailed by competition, as the Circumlocution Office. Dickens creates a devastating analysis out of lengthy exposition—by now he could risk making speeches in the novels—and very funny satirical portraiture. The Tite Barnacle family is animated

BLEAK HOUSE; from the engraving by 'Phiz'

LITTLE DORRIT: Maggy listens to Little Dorrit's 'Story of the Princess';
from the engraving by 'Phiz'

A TALE OF TWO CITIES: In Dr Manette's Soho garden: Dr Manette, Mr Lorry, Sidney Carton, Charles Darnay and Lucie Manette; from the engraving by 'Phiz'

OUR MUTUAL FRIEND: Silas Wegg, the evil Genius of the House of
Boffin; from the engraving by Marcus Stone

by ludicrous satire which rests on the solid basis of Dickens's introductory exegesis unfolding 'The Whole Science of Government'. After eleven paragraphs of expository satire Dickens feels free to use ridicule:

> He had a superior eye-glass dangling round his neck, but unfortunately had such flat orbits to his eyes, and such limp little eyelids, that it wouldn't stick in when he put it up, but kept tumbling out against his waistcoat buttons with a click that discomposed him very much.

The eyeglass and the limp little eyelids are part of the caricature of the affectation and feebleness of this ruling class, but there is the superfluous flight so dear to Dickens in the flat orbits of the eyes. The language has an accurate imitation of vagueness and polite exclamatoriness—many 'I says' and 'Look heres'—which are ridiculously punctuated by the business with the clicking eyeglass. Light comedy is certainly not an end in itself, and indeed the very lightness here is appropriate to the portraiture. The Tite Barnacles ought not to be so flimsy and silly, ought not to be figures of Dickensian fun. The levity is part of reproach and bitter criticism, but it is also typical of *Little Dorrit's* less tense, grim, and enclosed satiric world. It would be hard to imagine Flora Finching and her Aunt, for instance, in *Bleak House*.

But as in *Bleak House* the comic is often neighbour to the grim or pathetic feeling. In *Bleak House* we pass innocently from chat about tainted chops to the grisly scene of Spontaneous Combustion. In these last novels Dickens seems to be able to contaminate one feeling by another, so that we scarcely know whether to call the fun grisly or the horror the more macabre for the presence of laughter. Dickens's imagination was always attracted by rich mixtures of feeling, and the mixtures grow richer in the late novels. The suicide of Merdle, the financier whose soiled name, taken from *merde*, gives him away, is preluded by some light comedy of manners in Fanny's drawing-room. It must be remembered that Fanny is a recent graduate from prison:

'I thought I'd give you a call, you know.'

'Charmed, I am sure,' said Fanny.

'So I am off,' added Mr Merdle, getting up. 'Could you lend me a penknife?'

It was an odd thing, Fanny smilingly observed, for her who could seldom prevail upon herself even to write a letter, to lend to a man of such vast business as Mr Merdle. 'Isn't it?' Mr Merdle acquiesced; 'But I want one; and I know you have got several little wedding keepsakes about, with scissors and tweezers and such things in them. You shall have it back tomorrow.'

'Edmund,' said Mrs Sparkler, 'open (now, very carefully, I beg and beseech, for you are so very awkward) the mother-of-pearl box on my little table there, and give Mr Merdle the mother-of-pearl penknife.'

'Thank you,' said Mr Merdle; 'but if you have got one with a darker handle, I think I should prefer one with a darker handle.'

'Tortoise-shell?'

'Thank you,' said Mr Merdle; 'yes. I think I should prefer tortoise-shell.'

Undertaking not to get ink on the knife, he goes off to kill himself.

Both *Bleak House* and *Little Dorrit* are novels of multiple action, organized not only by central symbols but by an operatic intricacy of plot, which is slowly and mysteriously wound and rapidly unwound. As early as *Oliver Twist* and *Barnaby Rudge* Dickens had used complicated intrigue, mystery and unravelling, but in *Bleak House* and *Little Dorrit* such plots cover a huge range of characters, and the mystery and final revelation involve almost everyone of importance. Separate threads of action, character and society are gathered up in action as well as symbolism and subject, and the last curtain can be economically inclusive. The plot takes in the love-story, the criminal adventure and the satire on institutions. Dickens often creates a symbol which figures his structure as well as contributing to it: the symbol of the road which brings future acquaintances towards us, the images in the fire, or the echoing footsteps. The imagery of roads begins in the first chapter of *Little Dorrit* and the prison-keeper sings, 'Who passes by this road so late? Compagnon de la Majolaine', a suitable overture for a novel concerned with many journeys. Journeys in the late novels are not what they were in early Dickens, the action and motion of picaresque and episodic structure, but now form only a part, not the total trajectory, of action. The shadows of futurity, the anticipations of the future, the approaching strangers and the hysterically mounting echoes cast typically dark and ominous gloom in the dark novels.

A Tale of Two Cities (1859), contains not only this imagery of a dreadful future, in which we hear the gathering sound of the revolution, but something of the prison mood and claustrophobia of *Dorrit*. It is chiefly interesting for such feeling and atmosphere, and stands out, like *Barnaby Rudge* amongst the early novels, as a tale of action and adventure. It also stands out, as *Barnaby Rudge* does not, as a very feeble novel. It is bound together by symbolism and plot, has some interesting starts that go nowhere—the character of Dr Manette, for instance—no satiric or comic power, and very little character-interest. Its contemporaneity is plain in the fine opening oratory, and in its Carlylean inspiration and source. It is stark in moral action, simple in feeling, quite a good novel to read in childhood, but one which does not wear well into adult life. Its most characteristic defect is in its language. Like George Eliot's *Romola*, it suffers from the double artificiality of using the language of another time and another country. Dickens usually relies very heavily, both for comedy and character, on the colours of his language, and in this novel the characters' speech is stilted and characterless. Even where this is relieved by pseudo-translation from the French, of a mildly entertaining kind, the relief soon palls. There are some good passages, like the obsession of Manette or the knitting of Madame Defarge (another symbol of ominous futurity) and there is the good idea, which degenerates into mere plotting, of the physical likeness and moral unlikeness of Darnay and Carton. But the flatness and hollowness of character, and reliance on external action, make it very atypical of this period, and indeed of Dickens's work as a whole. It is properly bracketed with some of his feebly melodramatic stories which also lack density of language and character, and of which the story *Hunted Down* (1859) is a convenient instance.

This lapse is followed by *Great Expectations* (1861) which many people would claim is Dickens's best novel, and which is certainly remarkably dense, subtle and detailed in its dramatic psychology. It is a profound study of the person-ally-felt theme of the bad mother and the unloved child, which Edmund Wilson has brilliantly related to Dickens's own feelings of hostility and deprivation. Once more we have a solitary orphan, no longer the victim of impersonal institutions, but uncomfortably shuttling between the un-loving and effective Mrs Joe and the loving and ineffective Joe. The personal story is certainly not shut off from society, and it offers a complex analysis through psychology, plot, symbol and fable. The grotesque characters of Miss Havisham and Magwitch are brought together in a conflict of class and wealth which accumulates its psychological and symbolic force through many particulars. The plot is one of Dickens's best, at once intricate and lucid, highly original yet commanding the immediate assent of fable. Pip moves innocently into the convict's orbit of gratitude, need, ambition and power, when he first innocently and spon-taneously blesses the broken 'wittles' and hopes that Mag-witch is enjoying the stolen food. The convict chokes at the first words of hospitality and love he has ever heard, and Pip's life begins to be ironically re-made. At first he is formed not by Magwitch's money but by a growing class-consciousness which destroys the simple and spontaneous human warmth and generosity. When he in his turn is contemptuously fed like a dog in Miss Havisham's yard, he begins his hard education in class-antagonism and great expectations. This is the loss of innocence in a world where Dickens does not pretend to ignore social determinism; in a world where love requires the right manners, the right accent, the right clothes and the right income. Dickens sets up this world and explores it with irony and regret. Magwitch is the fairy godfather who pays for Pip's education and thus lets him act out the fantasy of becoming a gentleman who will please Estella. It is a novel where separate fantasies struggle and defeat each other: Miss Havisham's mad dream of creating a heartless girl who will act out her need for sexual revenge locks with the convict's fantasy of making the gentleman he can himself never be. The author locks together the plots of Magwitch and Miss Havisham and the intentions and fantasies cross. Magwitch has made a gentleman who cannot stand his table-manners, Miss Havisham finds that the destruction of the heart means that Estella can make no exception for her. Pip's discovery of his real benefactor is one of the best recognition scenes in Dickens, because its shocking release of tension is not only the result of the manipulation of ignorance, curiosity and suspicion, but also a moment of moral discovery. It leads to the conversion of Pip, to his forced intimacy with Magwitch, which, after all, becomes love.

Estella's education and perversion—a little like Louisa's— is shown from the outside, as is her eventual change of heart. Pip's is shown from the inside, in a confessional self-analysis in which he unbares his secret life and its causality. It is easy to overrate this analysis, simply because it is on a larger scale, and more detailed, than anything else in Dickens. But it has its weakness: Pip is really made too clearly and completely aware of the social and emotional forces that have made him what he is. His process and motivation are made available to him in a way that is not intrinsically implausible, but just not related to his individual limitations. It is a first-person novel that could really do with an omniscient author possessed of more wisdom than the hero. Pip is, moreover, not endowed with anything like the 'sensitive register of consciousness' which we find in, say, Maggie Tulliver or most of the central characters of Henry James.

He is not shown, like them, in a fine psychic notation which imitates the fantasy, reason and perception of the brain that feels and the heart that thinks. We do not see him breaking down old categories and emerging into new ones, like Maggie or James's Strether, in a process which does not break through into a final 'truth' but which only ends with life. This is, of course, an invidious comparison, but I make it in order to stress that this is a great psychological novel only by Dickens's standards. Here he explores the inner life of feeling and thinking more tenaciously and concentratedly than anywhere else, but it is not the kind of psychological novel which imitates the activity of the psyche. It describes the inner life, but does not dramatize it. There are a few exceptions, mostly in the descriptions of the child's sensations and feelings, but they are few.

Great Expectations, like *David Copperfield*, is a novel of memory, and as such blurs character and personality in a way both convenient and evasive. Pip's story is told through the medium of recollection, and Pip is not directly shown as an unpleasant and obtuse snob, but always seen through the memory, insight and sensibility of his older self. This makes his development and change of heart rather remote and shadowy, though there are some impressive moments of moral feeling, as when he suddenly sees himself in relation to Joe and Magwitch, as someone who has failed in love and loyalty. As so often in Dickens, the outline of development and conversion is firm and plain, the detail omitted. We see the moral action in the simple action of a fable: Pip is moved by seeing his opposite in Magwitch, his double in Estella; Miss Havisham is moved by recognizing in Pip a victim of love like herself. We tend to overlook the absence of a direct dramatization of the unregenerate Pip, and he is really much the same all the way through, imaginative, sensitive, self-critical, telling us but not showing us that he was different once. The places when the unconverted Pip shows through tend, not surprisingly, to be in dialogue, like the passage where he tries to tell Biddy that it would be a good thing if Joe could attempt some self-improvement. The first-person narrative is something Dickens never used quite happily.

One of the great successes of the novel, however, is its fusion of the individual story with the social indictment. Dickens shows in Pip the natural unconditioned life of the heart and the socially destructive process which weakens and distorts it, transforming instinct into calculation, human love into manipulation, generosity into greed, spontaneity into shame and ambition. Though it softens and sentimentalizes the class issue by the pastoral image of Joe and his forge which begs the whole question of determinism, it does produce some striking criticisms and ironies. The human centre is socially expressive. Pip's aspirations as he climbs to the top are endowed by the tainted money typical of his society, but the process and some of the social and emotional changes involved are still relevant as the meritocracy rises. Both Joe and Biddy are fairly free of patronizing presentation, have dignity and toughness, are not babies like Sleary, but inhabit the adult world. The end originally planned by Dickens would have kept Estella and Pip apart, though even this version reveals a strong optimism in Pip's ability to break with his social conditioning and start again, with the far from slight advantage of a good bourgeois education. But both the old and the revised endings show the modesty and lack of exclamatory climax of *Hard Times* and *Little Dorrit:* Pip and Estella are sad and scarred people, and the last words of the book remind us of darkness as well as light. Dickens simplifies the social issues, certainly, but the indictment remains, and what optimism we find cannot be called facile.

Our Mutual Friend (1865) is also a conversion story with social significance. It too deals with class, wealth and social mobility. Plot and moral action are tightly bound together, in a multiple action which takes us back to *Bleak House* and *Little Dorrit*. Like *Great Expectations*, it concerns a moral ordeal and test, though in this novel the test is set by the characters. The plot-makers within the novel are not frustrated, or perverse, or innocent, and they come out as rather flat, like Harmon Rokesmith, or as cosy caricatures, like the Boffins. Harmon stages the pseudo-conversion of Boffin, the Golden Dustman whose heart of gold becomes —Midaslike—chilled and hardened. This impersonated corruption acts as a test and a warning to Bella Wilfer, a nice girl with mercenary leanings. The false conversion brings about the true one. In this novel Dickens separates the subjects of money and class, dealing with them in different actions, though there is plenty of linking material in the chorus of Veneerings and Podsnaps. The story of Bella and the Boffins might have involved class but is simply a fable about love and money, while the story of Lizzie Harmon and her rival lovers deals expressly with problems of class, aspiration, conflict and division. Bradley Headstone, the repressed, respectable and passionate school-master is opposed to Eugene Wrayburn, the idle, *ennuyé*, able and perverse gentleman. Backed by Charlie, Lizzie's clever and ambitious brother, these characters act out a splendid *crime passionel* which is thickly detailed and documented as socially determined action.

The several mysteries, some overt, some covert, are less concentratedly unified than the action of *Bleak House:* there is the impersonation of Rokesmith by Harmon, the impersonation of a miser by Boffin, which goes back to *Martin Chuzzlewit*, the story of the crime, and rich supporting material, grotesque, comic, pathetic, and satiric. The best thing in the novel is the psychological study of crime, not exactly new in Dickens, who had long ago shown Sikes's solitude and guilt and fear in the fire, and listening to the cheapjack selling stain-remover, and, a little later, Jonas Chuzzlewit and his telltale heart, but new in its careful sociological backing. In the analysis of Bradley he moves out of the so-called 'criminal classes' to draw a new kind of meritocratic monster whose violence, repression and jealousy are part of a deadly struggle for respectability and

sexuality in a not very intelligent man of strong passions
with a need for social conformity. Dickens's method seems
deceptively simple, tending to socio-psychological analysis
on the one hand, and expressive stage-gestures like the
beating of a hand on a stone, on the other. But what is
admirable and very far from simple is the coherence of
thriller and social criticism, fused with that control of
contrary feelings which created the scene with the tortoise-
shell penknife. In the discovery scene in Bradley's schoolroom, for instance, Rogue Riderhood comes in the grimly
ridiculous guise of a friendly visitor wanting to put the
children through their paces. The well-drilled chorus of
children chirping their facts speaks fully for the education
which has shaped Bradley, and provides just the right kind
of thin surface of innocent routine on which Riderhood
can threateningly play and then violently break through,
after a tensely mounting examination not unlike his name-
sake Red Ridinghood's interrogation of the wolf.

But the novel as a whole lacks the control and unity of
such individual scenes. Despite the story of crime and
punishment, the character of Wrayburn, and the excellent
comedy of Wegg and Venus, a pair of bizarre Morality
grotesques, there is much flat and undeveloped action, soft-
ness of character, and an unsatisfactory relation between the
whole and its parts. Wrayburn marries Lizzie, perhaps
reflecting a new flexibility in social attitudes to marriage
between the classes, as Humphrey House suggests, though
with crucial stages in his conflict and decision blurred by
grave illness, and a symbolic rescue from death and the
river. His marriage is finally approved by Twemlow, a
choric character of some importance, a 'real' gentleman
amongst the *nouveaux riches*, and an interesting new stereo-
type created by Dickens, the *gentleman* with a heart of gold.
Although the novel is bristling with convincing social
victims like Charley Hexam and Bradley, its converted or
virtuous characters are very much less appropriately convincing. Dickens's densely documented analysis of Bradley

only shows up the dreaminess of such figures as Bella and the
Boffins, and even Eugene has to be helped over the tricky
area of decision by symbolic action. The striking and
impressive figures of the Podsnaps, the Lammles and the
Veneerings, act out their own little drama and thus become
much more than a comic chorus, creating a satiric action
which is much closer to Thackeray's powerful caricature
of a whole world, in *Vanity Fair*, than anything else in
Dickens. If *Bleak House* moves us through pity and disgust,
and *Little Dorrit* through ironic claustophobia, *Our Mutual
Friend* moves us through the sharpest and most strident
satire Dickens ever created. It is the satire which appears on
the margin of previous novels but which, to my mind, takes
over in this novel and creates a world in which the benevo-
lent softnesses of Mr Wilfer the Cherub, and Bella's baby
and Wrayburn's marriage, and little Johnny's words in the
Children's Hospital about 'the boofer lady', simply shrivel
up before our eyes. The best that we can find in this world
is the likely alliance of the Lammles, taken in and making
the best of things, or of Jenny Wren, with her sustaining
fantasy of the father who is a child. Dickens creates such a
powerful anatomy of a corrupting and corrupted society,
ruled and moved by greed and ambition, that the wishful
filling fantasies of virtue and conversion are too fragile to
support faith. That contemptuous insight out of which he
drew Podsnap's humours and the grotesque dust-heaps
where the scavenging Wegg prods with his wooden leg is
realized in the concreteness of sensuous detail and appropriate language. Dickens can make virtue lisp like a baby or
rhapsodize like a saint, but it seldom speaks with the un-
erring individual tones of Podsnap's loud patronizing
complacency or the drunken ellipses of Dolls or the soaring
'tones of moral grandeur' of the Lammles' duet. Virtue
often speaks in the neutral language that expresses neither
personality nor class, as in Mrs Boffin or Lizzie, where style
is not only dead but also glosses over the social difficulties of
class and marriage. Boffin the miser is so much more sharply

incised in manners and speech—'Scrunch or be scrunched'—than Boffin the good old man, that it is not surprising that Gissing thought Dickens must have really intended to make the Golden Dustman a study in deterioration. Betty Higden is endowed with a certain life because she is given a language, and she is perhaps the most effective instance of virtuous energy in the book. The others are either nonentities or unappealing: Bella does not want to be the doll in the doll's house, but her marriage and maternity are nothing if not embarrassingly doll-like. Neither the action nor the psychology of individual goodness is strong enough to heal those sore spots shown and painfully touched in pity and violence and satire.

Dickens died in 1870, after six monthly parts of *Edwin Drood* had come out. This last novel begins as a more concentrated and specialized mystery story than anything else he wrote, and it is likely that the central interest would have developed from the contrast between John Jasper's respectable public life and his secret drug-taking criminality, perhaps related to the practices of the Thugs, in which there was some contemporary interest. Edmund Wilson gives a good account of those many scholarly speculations which naturally sprang up to complete a detective story left unfinished. It seems unwarrantable to suggest, as some have done, that Jasper is to be a study in dual personality, and I can see little in the suggestion that the detective, Datchery, is Helena Landless in disguise, but the novel's chief pleasure must lie in such guesses at riddles. It also has the interest of greatly muted language and character. It is probably the one Dickens novel from which one could quote passages not immediately recognizable as Dickensian; and two of its characters, Mr Gregious and Mr Crisparkle, are interesting serious treatments of eccentrics who would in an earlier novel have been more exaggeratedly comic: Dickens develops them steadily and respectfully, in an almost Trollopian combination of the serious and slightly comic portrait. But it is only a fragment, the unfinished novel of an author who wrote hand to mouth, even if with a sense of design.

IV. CONCLUSION

Some of the novels written in the second half of Dickens's career as a novelist are markedly different from each other, in form and quality, and many of their features are found in the earlier work too. But a study of these later novels brings out one characteristic feature which I want to dwell on in conclusion. This is Dickens's developing sense of character.

Robert Garis, in *The Dickens Theatre*, has discussed that frank and open theatricality with which Dickens presents and animates his work. Theatricality is a useful word to use of the vitality and flourish of his appearances as an author, and useful too in defining the limits of his art. We should insist on these limits not because Dickens has been over-praised, but in order to try to recognize his individuality. He is theatrical, for instance, in his use of external action. His stage is not often even the lonely stage of soliloquy, but a stage crowded with the lively, stereotyped, stagey, concrete, simplified, physically exciting actions of actors. Dickens provides not only script and stage-directions but movement and performances too. His novels are like plays in action. But in the last novels, perhaps going back a little earlier than *Bleak House* to *Dombey and Son* and *David Copperfield*, he seems to be pushing this theatrical and extrovert art beyond the limits of theatricality. The attempt to imply the inner life of characters begins with the repressions of Dombey and Edith, both shown stagily but subtly. It continues in the failure of Esther Summerson whom Dickens is trying to create from the inside, though often with the disastrous effect of making a reserved and introspective character behave like a self-conscious puppet, from the double pressure of being ideal heroine and story-teller. But *Bleak House* is a valiant failure in an attempt to show the inner life of a human being in one part of the novel, and the impersonal dramatized vision holding up a mirror to society, in the other. In *Hard Times* he places his analysis of the inner life, most courageously and effectively, in a very simple fable, and shows it, as in *Dombey and Son*, not through the technique of enlarged soliloquy, where he is generally weak, but through implication and reticence, where he is strong. The psychology becomes more complex and mobile in content as he goes on experimenting in form: in *Little Dorrit* we have the inner self of Clennam's vivid ordinariness, and Dickens moves from this success to others, in Pip and Wrayburn. He is exploring a kind of character really belonging to another kind of novel, very far from theatrical, that novel of inner action written by Charlotte Brontë, George Eliot, George Meredith and Henry James, where the very form of the novel takes on the imprint of consciousness. Dickens's persistent experiments are marked by a limitation. He is apparently not trying to write whole novels of inner action, but inserting this inner analysis of complexity into *his* kind of novel, placing its subtlety under the spotlight that glares on the Dickens stage. Sometimes he can only bring it off for short stretches, as with the childhood of David, sometimes he manages the marvellous sleight-of-hand that makes us feel we have had full access to the conflicts of Dombey, Edith, and Louisa. Sometimes he creates the dense particularity of Pip, Clennam, Wrayburn. But it is a dense particularity which can be revealed by his spotlight. And it keeps strange company, which is not complex, or dense, or always very individualized. It is the story of an inner life, rather than the presentation of an inner life.

It points to three things. First, to that theatrical and extrovert nature of his genius, in which he continued to write at different stages of ideology, vision and craft. Next, it reveals his delight in difficulty, in that strenuousness spoken of by Henry James, which shows itself so energetically in Dickens's attempt to push beyond the frontiers of his genius. Finally, it is no accident that in those novels where he succeeds in actualizing a centre of character, we feel least troubled by the duality and disparity of his analysis of the individual and the society. His developing interest in psychology seems at times to go against the grain of his genius, but in fact his sociological imagination needed the particulars of a sense of character, and is badly betrayed and isolated when Dickens fails to anatomize the human heart. It is that powerful sociological imagination which triumphs most truthfully when Dickens succeeds in piercing through to the inner life.

CHARLES DICKENS

A Select Bibliography

(Place of publication London, unless stated otherwise. Detailed bibliographical information will also be found in the appropriate volume of
The Cambridge Bibliography of English Literature and *Supplement.*)

Bibliography:

THE BIBLIOGRAPHY OF DICKENS: A bibliographical list arranged in
   chronological order of the published writings in prose and verse,
   (from 1834 to 1880), by G. H. Shepherd (1880).

DICKENSIANA: A bibliography of the literature relating to Charles
   Dickens and his writings, by F. G. Kitton (1886)

THE MINOR WRITINGS OF CHARLES DICKENS: A bibliography and sketch,
   by F. G. Kitton (1886)

THE FIRST EDITIONS OF THE WRITINGS OF CHARLES DICKENS AND THEIR
   VALUES: A bibliography, by J. C. Eckel (1903).
   —revised and enlarged edition, 1932. Mainly for collectors.

CHARLES DICKENS: An excerpt from the general catalogue of printed
   books in the British Museum (1926).

A BIBLIOGRAPHY OF THE PERIODICAL WORKS OF CHARLES DICKENS:
   Bibliographical, analytical, and statistical, by T. Hatton and
   A. H. Cleaver (1933)
   —mainly for collectors.

THE DICKENS STUDENT AND COLLECTOR, A list of writings relating to
   Charles Dickens and his works, 1836-1945, by W. Miller (1946).

VICTORIAN FICTION: A GUIDE TO RESEARCH, ed. L. Stevenson; Cambridge, Mass. (1963)
   —includes 'Dickens' by A. B. Nisbet: a discriminating and important
   critical survey.

VICTORIAN STUDIES: 'Victorian Bibliography' (in each annual, June
   number); Bloomington, Indiana
   —gives the best current bibliography of Dickens, including numerous
   and important articles on his work impossible to include below.

Collected Editions:

WORKS, 17 vols (1847-68)
   —the 'first cheap edition'.
LIBRARY EDITION, 22 vols (1858-9)
   —this was re-issued in thirty vols (1861-74) with new title pages.

41

THE CHARLES DICKENS EDITION, 21 vols (1867-[74]).

THE LETTERS OF CHARLES DICKENS, edited by his sister-in-law and eldest daughter [Georgina Hogarth and Mary Dickens], 3 vols (1880[1879]-1882).

THE SPEECHES OF CHARLES DICKENS: 1841-70. Edited and prefaced by R. H. Shepherd (1884)

—a re-arrangement of an edition put together in 1870. Incomplete and inaccurate.

THE WORKS, 20 vols (1892-1925). With Introductions by Charles Dickens the younger

—the Macmillan edition.

GADSHILL EDITION, ed. A. Lang, 36 vols (1897-[1908])

—including Dickens's *Miscellaneous Papers*, Vols XXXV and XXXVI, edited by B. W. Matz (1908), which mainly comprises his articles in *Household Words* and *All the Year Round* not collected in *Reprinted Pieces* and *The Uncommercial Traveller*, and others contributed to the *Examiner*, *Daily News*, *Cornhill*, etc. *The Miscellaneous Papers* were included in the National and Centenary Editions (1908 and 1911) and in the Nonesuch Edition (1938) under the title of *Collected Papers*. They have also been reprinted separately.

AUTHENTIC EDITION, 21 vols (1901-[06]).

OXFORD INDIA PAPER DICKENS, 17 vols (1901-2).

BIOGRAPHICAL EDITION, ed. A. Waugh, 20 vols (1902-3).

NATIONAL EDITION, 40 vols (1906-8).

CENTENARY EDITION, 36 vols (1910-11).

THE WAVERLEY EDITION, 30 vols (1913-15)

—with introductions by well-known authors, including one by G. B. Shaw on *Hard Times*.

MR AND MRS CHARLES DICKENS: His letters to Her, ed. W. Dexter (1935)

—not included in the Nonesuch Edition, 1938.

THE NONESUCH DICKENS ed. A. Waugh, W. Dexter, T. Hatton, and H. Walpole, 23 vols (1937-8)

—this includes the *Letters of Charles Dickens*, ed. W. Dexter, three vols (1938). Although of great value as the fullest edition published so far, it is most incomplete and unreliable. It is being superseded by the Pilgrim edition.

LETTERS FROM CHARLES DICKENS TO ANGELA BURDETT-COUTTS, 1841-62, ed. E. Johnson (1953)

—also published as *The Heart of Charles Dickens*; New York (1952).

'New Letters of Charles Dickens to John Forster', ed. G. G. Grubb and K. J. Fielding. In *Boston University Studies in English*, II, 1956, 140–93.

NEW OXFORD ILLUSTRATED DICKENS, 21 vols (1947–59).

OXFORD DICKENS: general editors, J. Butt and K. Tillotson
—a new edition of Dickens's works, planned to present a revised text which takes into account original manuscripts, proofs and authors revisions. The first volume to appear (in 1966) was *Oliver Twist*, ed. K. Tillotson.

THE SPEECHES OF CHARLES DICKENS, ed. K. J. Fielding (1960)
—the definitive text; much more accurate and complete than earlier collections.

THE SELECTED LETTERS OF CHARLES DICKENS, ed. F. W. Dupee; New York (1960)
—with a fair introduction, but the letters are familiar reprints.

THE LETTERS OF CHARLES DICKENS (THE PILGRIM EDITION) ed. M. House and G. Storey (1965, in progress). *Volume One*, 1820–1839, with associate-editors W. J. Carlton, P. Collins, K. J. Fielding, and K. Tillotson (1965). There will probably be twelve volumes in all which will give the definitive text approximately 12,000 letters. Essential.

Note: Most of the MSS of the novels are in the Forster Collection at the Victoria and Albert Museum, London. There are other major MSS collections in the Pierpoint Morgan Library, New York, and the Henry E. Huntington Library, San Marino, California.

Separate Works:

SUNDAY UNDER THREE HEADS: As it is; as Sabbath Bills would make it; as it might be made (1836). *Essay*
—published under the pseudonym 'Timothy Sparks'.

SKETCHES BY 'BOZ': Illustrative of every-day life, and every-day people, 2 vols (1836). *Essays*
—a second series in one volume appeared at the end of 1836, and the whole series in one volume (1839).

THE VILLAGE COQUETTES: a comic opera (1836). *Libretto*

THE POSTHUMOUS PAPERS OF THE PICKWICK CLUB, containing a faithful record of the perambulations, perils, travels, adventures, and sporting transactions of the corresponding members. Edited by 'Boz' (1837). *Novel*

—all Dickens's novels published in monthly numbers between 1836 and 1866 appeared in twenty parts of thirty-two pages; Numbers XIX and XX, however, were always issued together as a so-called 'double number' of only forty-eight pages. *Pickwick* was published from April 1836 to November 1837.

THE STRANGE GENTLEMAN; a comic burletta, in two acts (1837). *Drama*

—based on 'The Great Winglebury Duel' in *Sketches by 'Boz'*.

IS SHE HIS WIFE? OR SOMETHING SINGULAR: a comic burletta in one act (1837). *Drama*

SKETCHES OF YOUNG GENTLEMEN: dedicated to the young ladies (1838). *Essays*

—published anonymously.

OLIVER TWIST; or, the parish boy's progress, 3 vols (1838). *Novel*

—first published in *Bentley's Miscellany* as a monthly serial between February 1837 and March 1839.

THE LIFE AND ADVENTURES OF NICHOLAS NICKLEBY: containing a faithful account of the fortunes, misfortunes, uprisings, down-fallings, and complete career of the Nickleby family (1839). *Novel*

—first issued in twenty (as nineteen) monthly parts from April 1838.

SKETCHES OF YOUNG COUPLES: with an urgent remonstrance to the gentlemen of England (being bachelors or widowers), on the present alarming crisis (1840). *Essays*

—published anonymously.

MASTER HUMPHREY'S CLOCK, 3 vols (1840-1). *Novels, sketches, and short stories*

—originally issued in eighty-eight weekly parts, and also in monthly numbers, from 4 April 1840.

THE OLD CURIOSITY SHOP (1841)

—in the *Clock* from 25 April 1840.

BARNABY RUDGE: a tale of the riots of 'eighty (1841). *Novel*

—in the *Clock* from 13 February 1841.

AMERICAN NOTES, for general circulation, 2 vols (1842). *Travel*

THE LIFE AND ADVENTURES OF MARTIN CHUZZLEWIT: his relatives, friends, and enemies. Comprising all his wiles and his ways, with an historical record of what he did, and what he didn't; showing, moreover, who inherited the family plate, who came in for the silver spoons, and who for the wooden ladles. This whole forming a complete key to the house of Chuzzlewit (1844). *Novel*

—first issued in twenty (as nineteen) monthly parts from January 1843.

A CHRISTMAS CAROL: In prose. Being a ghost story of Christmas (1843). *Short Story*

—the first of the Christmas books.

THE CHIMES: a goblin story of some bells that rang an old year out and a new year in (1844). *Short Story*.

THE CRICKET ON THE HEARTH: a fairy tale of home (1845). *Short Story*

THE BATTLE OF LIFE: a love story (1846). *Short Story*

PICTURES FROM ITALY (1846). *Travel*

—first published in the *Daily News* between 21 January and 2 March 1846, with some variations, as seven 'Travelling Letters'.

DEALINGS WITH THE FIRM OF DOMBEY AND SON, WHOLESALE, RETAIL, AND FOR EXPORTATION (1848). *Novel*

—first issued in twenty (as nineteen) monthly parts from October 1846.

THE HAUNTED MAN AND THE GHOST'S BARGAIN: a fancy for Christmas time (1848). *Short Story*

THE PERSONAL HISTORY, ADVENTURES, EXPERIENCES, AND OBSERVATION OF DAVID COPPERFIELD THE YOUNGER OF BLUNDERSTONE ROOKERY (Which he never meant to be published on any account) (1850). *Novel*

—first issued in twenty (as nineteen) monthly parts from May 1849.

CHRISTMAS STORIES (1850-67). *Short Stories*

—published as part of the Christmas numbers of *Household Words* and *All the Year Round* between 1850 and 1867, usually written either in collaboration with Wilkie Collins or in conjunction with other regular contributors.

A CHILD'S HISTORY OF ENGLAND, 3 vols (1852, 1853, 1854). *History*

—first published in *Household Words* between 25 January 1851 and 10 December 1853.

BLEAK HOUSE (1853). *Novel*

—first issued in twenty (as nineteen) monthly parts, from March 1852.

HARD TIMES: For these times (1854). *Novel*

—first published in *Household Words* in weekly instalments from 1 April to 12 August.

LITTLE DORRIT (1857). *Novel*

—first issued in twenty (as nineteen) monthly parts from December 1855.

THE LAZY TOUR OF TWO IDLE APPRENTICES (1857). *Travel*

—in collaboration with Wilkie Collins. First published in *Household Words*, 3 October to 31 October 1857.

REPRINTED PIECES (1858). *Essays*

—first appeared in book form as part of Vol. 8 of the Library Edition of the collected works. Consists of thirty-one articles contributed to *Household Words*.

A TALE OF TWO CITIES (1859). *Novel*

—first published in *All the Year Round* in weekly instalments from 30 April to 26 November.

HUNTED DOWN (1859). *Short Story*

—first published in the *New York Ledger* of 20 and 27 August, and 3 September 1859; also in *All the Year Round*, 4 and 11 August 1860.

GREAT EXPECTATIONS, 3 vols (1861). *Novel*

—first published in *All the Year Round* in weekly instalments from 1 December 1860 to 3 August 1861.

THE UNCOMMERCIAL TRAVELLER (1861). *Essays*

—a series of essays from *All the Year Round*; the first edition (1861) included seventeen papers; the next (1868) had an additional eleven; a further eight were added to the volume in an Illustrated Library Edition (1875); and one more, making thirty-seven altogether, to the Gadshill Edition (1908).

OUR MUTUAL FRIEND, 2 vols (1865). *Novel*

—first issued in twenty (as nineteen) monthly parts from May 1864.

GEORGE SILVERMAN'S EXPLANATION (1868). *Short Story*

—first published in the *Atlantic Monthly*, Boston, January to March 1868, also in *All the Year Round*, 1, 15 and 29 February 1868.

HOLIDAY ROMANCE (1868). *Children's Story*

—first published in *Our Young Folks*, Boston, between January and May 1868: also in *All the Year Round* between 25 January and 4 April 1868.

THE MYSTERY OF EDWIN DROOD (1870). *Novel*

—unfinished at Dickens's death. First issued in six monthly parts from April to September 1870; originally designed to be completed in twelve.

THE LAMPLIGHTER: A FARCE BY CHARLES DICKENS, 1838: Now first printed from a manuscript in the Forster Collection at the Victoria and Albert Museum (1879). *Drama*

THE LIFE OF OUR LORD: Written expressly for his children by Charles Dickens (1834). *Religion*
—not designed for publication.

Note: After reporting for *The Mirror of Parliament* and the *TrueSun*, Dickens was engaged on the *Morning Chronicle* from August 1834 to November 1836. He edited *Bentley's Miscellany* from January 1837 to February 1839; *The Daily News* from 21 January to 9 February 1846; *Household Words* from March 1850 to May 1859; and *All the Year Round* from April 1859 until his death. The original 'Office Book' of *Household Words*, recording author and payment for each article, is now in the Princeton University Library. See *Princeton University Library Chronicle*, Autumn, 1964. There are also a number of typescript copies—as at the Dickens House, 48 Doughty Street, London, WC1. There is no similar record for *All the Year Round*.

Some Critical and Biographical Studies:

DICKENS IN RELATION TO CRITICISM, by G. H. Lewes. *Fortnightly Review*, February 1872, 141-54.

THE LIFE OF CHARLES DICKENS, by J. Forster, 3 vols (1872, 1873, 1874)
—revised edition, in two volumes, 1876. The most useful edition is by J. W. T. Ley in one volume, 1928, which contains much additional material.

LITERARY STUDIES, by W. Bagehot (1879)
—includes a study of Dickens, Vol. II, 184-220, previously published in the *National Review*, October 1858, 458-86.

DICKENS, by A. W. Ward (1882).

THE CHILDHOOD AND YOUTH OF CHARLES DICKENS, by R. Langton. Manchester (1883)
—new edition, with additional material 1891.

CHARLES DICKENS AS I KNEW HIM, by G. Dolby (1885)
—the story of his reading tours in Great Britain and America (1866-70).

CHARLES DICKENS: By his eldest daughter, by M. Dickens (1885)
—re-worded as *My Father as I Recall Him* (1896).

CHARLES DICKENS BY PEN AND PENCIL, with Supplement, by F. G. Kitton (1890).

CHARLES DICKENS: A CRITICAL STUDY, by G. Gissing (1898).

CHARLES DICKENS: HIS LIFE, WRITINGS, AND PERSONALITY, by F. G. Kitton (1902).

THE DICKENSIAN, (1905, in progress)
—a magazine for Dickens lovers and a record of the Dickens Fellowship. Now published three times a year. Includes much of value.

CHARLES DICKENS, by G. K. Chesterton (1906).

CHARLES DICKENS, THE APOSTLE OF THE PEOPLE, by E. Pugh (1908).

DICKENS AND THE DRAMA, by S. J. A. Fitzgerald (1910).

APPRECIATIONS AND CRITICISMS OF THE WORKS OF CHARLES DICKENS, by G. K. Chesterton (1911).

THE CHARLES DICKENS ORIGINALS, by E. Pugh (1912).

CHARLES DICKENS, SOCIAL REFORMER, by W. W. Crotch (1913).

MEMOIRS OF CHARLES DICKENS, by P. H. Fitzgerald (1913).

CHARLES DICKENS, by A. C. Swinburne (1913).

THE DICKENS CIRCLE, by J. W. T. Ley (1918)
—a narrative of the novelist's friendships.

DICKENS AND THACKERAY, by O. Elton (1925)
—reprinted, with some additions, from the author's *Survey of English Literature (1830-80)* (1920).

THE IMMORTAL DICKENS, by G. Gissing (1925)
—introductions to the unfinished Rochester editions.

CHARLES DICKENS AND OTHER VICTORIANS, by Sir A. Quiller-Couch (1925).

CHARLES DICKENS, SHORTHAND WRITER, by W. J. Carlton (1926)
—Dickens as a reporter.

ÉTUDES ANGLAISES, by A. Maurois; Paris (1927)
—the first part of this volume was published in English translation as *Dickens* (1934).

MEMORIES OF MY FATHER, by Sir H. F. Dickens (1928).

DICKENS: a portrait in pencil, by R. Straus (1928)
—reprinted as *A Portrait of Dickens* (1938).

CHARLES DICKENS AS A LEGAL HISTORIAN, by W. S. Holdsworth; New Haven, Conn. (1928).

THE MAN CHARLES DICKENS, A VICTORIAN PORTRAIT, by E. Wagenknecht; Boston and New York (1929)
—revised with additions, 1966.

DICKENS, by B. Darwin (1933).

CHARLES DICKENS, HIS LIFE AND WORK, by S. Leacock (1933)

THE LIFE AND CHARACTER OF CHARLES DICKENS, by H. C. Dent (1933).

EARLY VICTORIAN NOVELISTS, by Lord D. Cecil (1934)
—contains a chapter on Dickens.

THE SENTIMENTAL JOURNEY. A life of Charles Dickens, by 'Hugh Kingsmill' [H. K. Lunn] (1934).

THE LIFE OF CHARLES DICKENS, by T. Wright (1935).

THOMAS WRIGHT OF OLNEY. An Autobiography (1936)

—Chapter 14, sub-titled 'A Startling Story. New Discoveries Respecting Charles Dickens, Respecting his Life at Nunhead . . .'

CHARLES DICKENS: the progress of a radical, by T. A. Jackson (1937).

DICKENS AND DAUGHTER, by G. Storey (1939).

DICKENS' WORKS IN GERMANY, 1837-1937, by E. N. Gummer (1940).

INSIDE THE WHALE AND OTHER ESSAYS, by G. Orwell (1940)

—includes 'Charles Dickens' reprinted in *Critical Essays*, 1946. Essential.

THE WOUND AND THE BOW: SEVEN STUDIES IN LITERATURE, by E. Wilson; Cambridge, Mass. (1941)

—includes 'Dickens: The Two Scrooges'. Still essential.

THE DICKENS WORLD, by A. H. House (1941)

—an important assessment.

CHARLES DICKENS, 1812-70, by U. Pope-Hennessy (1945).

Introduction to GREAT EXPECTATIONS contributed by G. B. Shaw, in the Novel Library (1947)

—Shaw's criticism is always stimulating though sometimes impossible to accept. There are many references to Dickens throughout his writings.

DICKENS: HIS CHARACTER, COMEDY, AND CAREER, by H. Pearson (1949).

CHARLES DICKENS: A BIOGRAPHICAL AND CRITICAL STUDY, by J. Lindsay (1950).

THE GREAT TRADITION, by F. R. Leavis (1950)

—includes 'Hard Times: an Analytical Note'. Its conclusions were more generally applicable to the other works than the author seemed willing to admit.

CHARLES DICKENS, by J. Symons (1951).

CHARLES DICKENS, HIS TRAGEDY AND TRIUMPH, by E. Johnson; New York (1953)

—the best biography since Forster's of 1872-4. New edition, 1965.

DICKENS AND ELLEN TERNAN, by A. B. Nisbet; Berkeley, California (1952) and Cambridge (1953)

—included important new material.

DICKENS ROMANCIER, by S. Monod; Paris (1953)

—an important study of Dickens's methods as a novelist.

NOVELS OF THE EIGHTEEN-FORTIES, by K. Tillotson (1954)

—particularly *Dombey and Son*.

ALL IN DUE TIME, by A. H. House (1955)
—includes 'Part Three: Dickens'.

DICKENS AND HIS READERS, Aspects of Novel-Criticism since 1836, by
G. H. Ford; Princeton (1955).

PHIZ: ILLUSTRATIONS FROM THE NOVELS OF CHARLES DICKENS: by A.
Johannsen; Chicago (1956)
—an interesting examination of minor variants in the engravings in
first editions.

GEORGINA HOGARTH AND THE DICKENS CIRCLE, by A. A. Adrian (1957)
—a useful and scholarly study.

CHARLES DICKENS, A CRITICAL INTRODUCTION, by K. J. Fielding (1957)
—revised and much enlarged, 1964.

CRAFT AND CHARACTER IN MODERN FICTION, by M. D. Zabel (1957)
—includes 'Dickens' in Part I, pp. 3-69.

DICKENS AT WORK, by J. Butt and K. Tillotson (1957).

CHARLES DICKENS, by S. Monod; Paris (1958)
—an illustrated introduction to Dickens, including a selection of
passages translated into French. Monod has also translated, edited
and introduced several of Dickens's novels.

CHARLES DICKENS, THE WORLD OF HIS NOVELS, by J. H. Miller; Cambridge, Mass. (1958)
—stimulating and thoughtful.

CHARLES DICKENS AND APPROPRIATE LANGUAGE, by R. Quirk; Durham
(1959)
—an inaugural lecture full of interesting stylistic comments.

THE MATURITY OF DICKENS, by M. Engel; Cambridge, Mass. (1959).

DICKENS INCOGNITO, by F. Aylmer (1959)
—about Dickens and Ellen Ternan. Definitely misleading as based
on an admitted mis-reading of certain records: see *Sunday Times*,
13 December 1959. Not to be completely ignored.

DICKENS ON EDUCATION, by J. Manning; Toronto (1959)
—useful, but not the last word.

CHARLES DICKENS: A PICTORIAL BIOGRAPHY, by J. B. Priestley (1961)
—full of interesting illustrative material.

THE IMAGINATION OF CHARLES DICKENS, by A. O. J. Cockshut (1961)
—well argued and thoughtful.

THE DICKENS CRITICS, ed. G. Ford and L. Lane Jr.; Ithaca, N.Y.
(1961)
—an extremely useful selection of critical studies from Poe to Angus
Wilson.

DISCUSSIONS OF CHARLES DICKENS, ed. W. Clark Rose; Boston (1961)
—a useful slim selection of previously published essays by current critics.

A Review of English Literature, Vol. II, No 3 (1961)
—a Dickens symposium, ed. J. Butt.

DICKENS AND THE TWENTIETH CENTURY, ed. J. Gross and G. Pearson (1962)
—twenty, mainly new, essays giving a fresh survey of the novels.

DICKENS AND CRIME, by P. A. W. Collins (1962)
—an interesting work of scholarship offering new insights if applied to biography and criticism.

DICKENS AND KAFKA, by M. Spilka; Bloomington, Indiana (1962)
—more Kafkan than Dickensian; it yields rewardingly to close study.

DOMBEY AND SON, by F. R. Leavis, *Sewanee Review*, LXX, 177-201 (1962)
—re-affirms the author's recognition of the 'inexhaustibly wonderful poetic life' in Dickens's prose.

DICKENS CRITICISM, A SYMPOSIUM, with G. H. Ford, E. Johnson, J. Hillis Miller, S. Monod, ed. N. Peyrouton; Cambridge, Mass. (1962)
—a useful, forward-looking survey.

DICKENS IN HIS TIME, by I. Brown (1963).

DICKENS AND EDUCATION, by P. A. W. Collins (1963)
—includes valuable new information and insight.

THE FLINT AND THE FLAME: THE ARTISTRY OF CHARLES DICKENS, by E. Davis; Columbia, Missouri (1963).

THE NEWGATE NOVEL 1830-1847, Bulwer, Ainsworth, Dickens and Thackeray, by K. Hollingsworth; Detroit (1963).

THE DROOD CASE, by F. Aylmer (1964)
—ingenious.

DICKENS STUDIES, ed. N. Peyrouton; Emerson College, Boston (1965, in progress)
—originally published three times a year but now twice yearly.

THE DICKENS THEATRE. A Re-Assessment of the novels, by R. Garis (1965)
—a critical work of distinction.

DICKENS FROM PICKWICK TO DOMBEY, by S. Marcus; New York (1965)
—an informed and persuasive, if uneven, commentary.

THE CHARLES DICKENS COMPENDIUM, by M. and M. Hardwick (1965)
—an informative compendium.

DICKENS: THE DREAMER'S STANCE, by T. Stoehr; Ithaca, N.Y. (1965).

DICKENS AND THE SCANDALMONGERS, Essays in Criticism, by E. Wagenknecht; Norman, Oklahoma (1965).

CIRCLE OF FIRE, by W. F. Axton; Lexington, Kentucky (1966)

CHARLES DICKENS AS A SERIAL NOVELIST, by A. C. Coolidge; Ames, Iowa (1966)

THE MAKING OF CHARLES DICKENS, by C. Hibbert (1967)

—the formative influence on his life up to 1836.

WRITERS AND THEIR WORK

General Editor: GEOFFREY BULLOUGH

The first 55 issues in the Series appeared under the General Editorship of T. O. BEACHCROFT
Issues 56-169 appeared under the General Editorship of BONAMY DOBRÉE

THE BRONTË SISTERS: P. Bentley
BROWNING: John Bryson
E. B. BROWNING: Alethea Hayter
SAMUEL BUTLER: G. D. H. Cole
BYRON: Herbert Read
CARLYLE: David Gascoyne
LEWIS CARROLL: Derek Hudson
CLOUGH: Isobel Armstrong
COLERIDGE: Kathleen Raine
CREEVEY & GREVILLE: J. Richardson
DE QUINCEY: Hugh Sykes Davies
DICKENS: K. J. Fielding
DICKENS: THE EARLY NOVELS:
                            Trevor Blount
DISRAELI: Paul Bloomfield
GEORGE ELIOT: Lettice Cooper
FERRIER & GALT: W. M. Parker
FITZGERALD: Joanna Richardson
MRS GASKELL: Miriam Allott
GISSING: A. C. Ward
THOMAS HARDY: R. A. Scott-James
                    and C. Day Lewis
HAZLITT: J. B. Priestley
HOOD: Laurence Brander
G. M. HOPKINS: Geoffrey Grigson
T. H. HUXLEY: William Irvine
KEATS: Edmund Blunden
LAMB: Edmund Blunden
LANDOR: G. Rostrevor Hamilton
EDWARD LEAR: Joanna Richardson
MACAULAY: G. R. Potter
MEREDITH: Phyllis Bartlett
JOHN STUART MILL: M. Cranston
WILLIAM MORRIS: P. Henderson
NEWMAN: J. M. Cameron
PATER: Iain Fletcher
PEACOCK: J. I. M. Stewart
ROSSETTI: Oswald Doughty
CHRISTINA ROSSETTI: G. Battiscombe
RUSKIN: Peter Quennell
SIR WALTER SCOTT: Ian Jack
SHELLEY: Stephen Spender
SOUTHEY: Geoffrey Carnall
R. L. STEVENSON: G. B. Stern
SWINBURNE: H. J. C. Grierson
TENNYSON: F. L. Lucas
THACKERAY: Laurence Brander
FRANCIS THOMPSON: P. Butter
TROLLOPE: Hugh Sykes Davies
OSCAR WILDE: James Laver
WORDSWORTH: Helen Darbishire

Twentieth Century:
W. H. AUDEN: Richard Hoggart
HILAIRE BELLOC: Renée Haynes
ARNOLD BENNETT: F. Swinnerton
EDMUND BLUNDEN: Alec M. Hardie
ELIZABETH BOWEN: Jocelyn Brooke
ROBERT BRIDGES: J. Sparrow
ROY CAMPBELL: David Wright

JOYCE CARY: Walter Allen
G. K. CHESTERTON: C. Hollis
WINSTON CHURCHILL: John Connell
R. G. COLLINGWOOD: E. W. F. Tomlin
I. COMPTON-BURNETT: P. H. Johnson
JOSEPH CONRAD: Oliver Warner
WALTER DE LA MARE: K. Hopkins
NORMAN DOUGLAS: Ian Greenlees
T. S. ELIOT: M. C. Bradbrook
FIRBANK & BETJEMAN: J. Brooke
FORD MADOX FORD: Kenneth Young
E. M. FORSTER: Rex Warner
CHRISTOPHER FRY: Derek Stanford
JOHN GALSWORTHY: R. H. Mottram
ROBERT GRAVES: M. Seymour-Smith
GRAHAM GREENE: Francis Wyndham
L. P. HARTLEY & ANTHONY POWELL:
        P. Bloomfield and B. Bergonzi
A. E. HOUSMAN: Ian Scott-Kilvert
ALDOUS HUXLEY: Jocelyn Brooke
HENRY JAMES: Michael Swan
JAMES JOYCE: J. I. M. Stewart
RUDYARD KIPLING: Bonamy Dobrée
D. H. LAWRENCE: Kenneth Young
C. DAY LEWIS: Clifford Dyment
WYNDHAM LEWIS: E. W. F. Tomlin
COMPTON MACKENZIE: K. Young
LOUIS MACNEICE: John Press
KATHERINE MANSFIELD: Ian Gordon
JOHN MASEFIELD: L. A. G. Strong
SOMERSET MAUGHAM: J. Brophy
GEORGE MOORE: A. Norman Jeffares
EDWIN MUIR: J. C. Hall
J. MIDDLETON MURRY: Philip Mairet
SEAN O'CASEY: W. A. Armstrong
GEORGE ORWELL: Tom Hopkinson
POETS OF 1939–45 WAR: R. N. Currey
POWYS BROTHERS: R. C. Churchill
J. B. PRIESTLEY: Ivor Brown
HERBERT READ: Francis Berry
FOUR REALIST NOVELISTS: V. Brome
BERNARD SHAW: A. C. Ward
EDITH SITWELL: John Lehmann
OSBERT SITWELL: Roger Fulford
KENNETH SLESSOR: C. Semmler
C. P. SNOW: William Cooper
STRACHEY: R. A. Scott-James
SYNGE & LADY GREGORY: E. Coxhead
DYLAN THOMAS: G. S. Fraser
EDWARD THOMAS: Vernon Scannell
G. M. TREVELYAN: J. H. Plumb
WAR POETS: 1914–18: E. Blunden
EVELYN WAUGH: Christopher Hollis
H. G. WELLS: Montgomery Belgion
PATRICK WHITE: R. F. Brissenden
CHARLES WILLIAMS: J. Heath-Stubbs
VIRGINIA WOOLF: B. Blackstone
W. B. YEATS: G. S. Fraser
ANDREW YOUNG & R. S. THOMAS:
        L. Clark and R. G. Thomas